The *Gospel* of *Thomas*

THE ORIGINAL SAYINGS OF JESUS

FROM THE WRITINGS OF

Jerome

STANSBURY
PUBLISHING
Chico, Ca.

The Gospel of Thomas:
The Original Sayings of Jesus
Copyright © 2018 by Jerome A. Dirnberger
First Edition

ISBN: 978-1-935807-43-8 paperback
ISBN: 978-1-935807-44-5 Kindle
ISBN: 978-1-935807-45-2 ePUB
Library of Congress Control Number:
2018958471

Stansbury Publishing is an imprint of
Heidelberg Graphics

Cover: stock photo copyright Zvonimir Atletic

This Book Is Dedicated To My Identical Twin Brother, Lawrence Andrew Dirnberger

1944–1967

St. Louis University High School, 1958–1962
University of Notre Dame, 1962–1966
US Marine Corp, 2nd Lt, 1966–1967

FOREWORD

The Gospel of Thomas starts by stating the sayings that follow are Jesus' words. I will come back to that later. Also, these sayings were recorded by Didymus Judas Thomas. *Didymus* means *twin* in Greek and *Thomas* is Aramaic for *twin*. And Judas we know from Mark 6:3 and Matthew 13:55 is Jesus' brother.

It is generally accepted now by biblical scholars that Judas is Jesus' twin brother. But also, by the Eastern Orthodox Church, he is Jesus' identical twin brother. This fact is beneficial for me in that I am also an identical twin (see prevous page). I believe this gives me some insights into being able to interpret this gospel into twenty-first century English.

More importantly, with Judas being

Jesus' twin, it gives his recording of the sayings greater credibility. He obviously heard them many times and might even helped develop them. So they are as authentic as other gospels, and maybe even more so.

In most translations (or interpretations) of Thomas' gospel, Thomas states they are "secret sayings." I believe "secret" does not convey the most accurate idea. For me, "difficult to understand" or "need for greater understanding" is optimum.

I spent my formal education at St. Louis University, Regis College in Denver, the University of Notre Dame, and the University of Colorado, specializing in early first century "Christianity" and continued this study afterwards on my own.

Introduction

This Manuscript

In 1945 near the Egyptian town of Nag Hammadi two farmers, Muhammed and Khalifa, found an earthen jar while digging for fertilizer. They broke open the jar and discovered 13 books containing manuscripts written in ancient Coptic. Included in this library, was a gospel purported to have been written by Thomas who was an apostle of the Jewish rabbi, Yesu of Nazareth. Also known as Yeshua in Aramaic and Jesus in English. This Gospel is a collection of 114 sayings (logia) of Jesus. While this manuscript has been translated into several languages, the original remains in Egypt at the Coptic Museum in Cairo.

Other Gospels

Well known are the four canonical Gospels: Matthew, Mark, Luke, and John. These books were written in the last half of the 1st century and probably not by the apostles whose names they are ascribed. Now the word "gospel" means "good news" in Greek, namely the good news that was spoken by Jesus in his message. In 185 CE Bishop Irenaeus decides his theology is what should define Christianity so he states these four gospels are the only true ones and all others are heretical and have to be burned. Thus the beginning of the New Testament was formed.

Currently there is a couple dozen other known gospels. Some are complete and others are only fragments. In general, each gospel is a variation of Christian theology with a specific focus. For example, in Matthew Jesus is the Messiah and in John Jesus is the Son of God. With regard to Mark, there are nine different versions with the shortest ending being at the empty tomb. Some gospels even have translation errors. For example: in Matthew 19:20-26 "camel" should be "rope" and Matthew 1:22 "virgin" should be "young woman." But each gospel has elements of truth and some real historical events related to Jesus and the Christian movement.

Background History

Since the time of Alexander the Great, Greek culture was a part of the Galilean way of life.

In 40 BCE Rome installed Herod the Great over the Jews in Palestine. He was a patron of the Greco-Roman culture. At his death, his son Herod Antipas ruled during most of Jesus' life.

Around 20 CE, Herod expanded the city of Sepphoris, near Nazareth, and re-named the city Sepphoris Autocratoris, in honor of the Emperor Tiberias.

While the rural villages in Galilee were mostly conservative Jewish with a few Gentiles in the population, it was the larger city of Sepphoris Autocratoris which was influenced by the Roman political structure, Greek culture and Herodian social elite. Jesus who lived and worked near this junction of two major trading routes would have been exposed to many different ethnic peoples and their beliefs.

Another important village for Jesus was Capernaum which was situated on the north shore of the Sea of Galilee. It would have been mainly a fishing village similar to many others around the Sea. Agriculture would also have added income to the local economy as archaeologists have found the remnants of oil and grain mills.

Jesus was a Jew and his religion was Judaism. He grew up learning to be a tradesman like his father and they lived in the small village of Nazareth. His mother, Mary, married Joseph and they had five sons including Jesus and probably two or more sisters (Mark 6:3, Luke 4:22, Matthew 13:55, Acts1:14).

He was very close with his father and, in fact, he called his personal God *abba* which means *dad*. This is unique to Jesus as there is no record of any previous Jewish rabbis using Abba to address their monotheistic God. It should be noted that in Jesus' message of praying he taught his followers to use the phrase: "our Father in Heaven..." He was also very close with his mother as she traveled with him when he was a rabbi. She was with him when he was tortured and crucified.

He was literate, thoughtful, creative, determined, and compassionate. As he said many times, he considered himself a rebel or reformer. He hated the bureaucracy of the Jewish religion and its power base. This fact in essence got him killed.

The historian Josephus, in his *Testimonium Flavianum* (book 18, chapter 3) said this about Jesus: "Now there was about this time Jesus, a wise man. For he was a doer of startling deeds, a teacher of such men as receive the truth with pleasure. And he gained a following both among many Jews and many of Greek origin. And when Pilate, at the suggestion of the principal men amongst us, condemned him to the cross, those that loved him at the first did not forsake him. And the tribe of Christians, so named from him, are not extinct at this day."

Jesus had a more elevated view of the status of women than was generally accorded them in the patriarchal society of the time as he also does with children who were expected to be silent. Jesus was sympathetic to the outcasts and marginal persons in society. The poor were an important group as he wanted people to forgive others debts. He wanted the poor to not be so anxious nor fret about their needs as God would provide. Jesus rejected the concept of impurity as he had contact with lepers, sinners, gentiles and the dead.

Who Influenced Jesus?

John the Baptist had great influence on helping Jesus develop his philosophy, vision and message probably more than anyone. Jesus was a loyal follower and took over John's ministry when he was arrested by Herod and put to death.

Flavius Josephus in his *Antiquities of the Jews*, book 18, chapter 5.2 says this about the Baptist: "... John, that was called the Baptist ... for Herod slew him, who was a good man, and commanded the Jews to exercise virtue, both as to righteousness towards one another, and piety towards God, and so to come to baptism; for that the washing [with water] would be acceptable to him, if they made use of it, not in order to the putting away [or the remission] of some sins [only], but for the purification of the body; supposing still that the soul was thoroughly purified beforehand by righteousness. Now when [many] others came in crowds about him, for they were very greatly moved [or pleased] by hearing his words. ..."

Jesus had a twin brother, Judas (Jude), who went by the nickname of Thomas (twin) and followed Jesus during his ministry. He wrote down Jesus' sayings in the Gospel of Thomas. His brother, James, was an apostle like Thomas. Mary, his mother, and a sister, also known as Mary, were part of the loyal followers called disciples. After Jesus' death, James became the leader of the "Christian" movement in Jerusalem.

Another loyal follower was Mary of Magdala who not only helped finance Jesus' ministry but became a confidant to him. They were considered by many to be intimate companions. She probably understood Jesus' vision and message better than the illiterate apostles. After Jesus' death, she helped them to the point that she was called the "apostle to the apostles." (ref: the Gospel of Philip and the Gospel of Mary)

Jesus' Speaking Style

Jesus' style was to refuse to give straightforward answers. Even though his disciples kept asking for explanations. His unique sayings are the beatitudes, those about turning the other cheek after being struck and the injunction to respect your enemies. To "treat people in the way you want to be treated" is closest in summarizing Jesus' perspective.

Jesus' sayings, aphorisms, and parables are unique to him as they:

- Cut against the social and religious grain

- Use surprise and shock

- Call for a reversal of roles

- Cannot be taken literally

- Force the listeners to think critically

- Have several levels of meaning

- Contain short and memorable phrases

- Do not invoke scripture to justify his pronouncements

- Challenge social boundaries

Jesus does not as a rule initiate dialogue or debate, nor does he offer to cure people. He rarely makes pronouncements or speaks about himself in the first person. He makes no claim to be the Anointed, the messiah. He is self-effacing, modest and unostentatious. He does not initiate debates nor controversies. He is passive until a question is put to him. He admonishes his followers to be servants of everyone. He urges humility as the cardinal virtue by both word and example. But he likes to eat and drink as he enjoyed weddings.

Jesus' Message ... Father and Kingdom of the Father

Jesus spoke most characteristically of God's Realm or Kingdom of God as close or already present but unrecognized. Jesus' God was symbolized as Father. He did not make predictions about the end of time. God was so real for him that he could not distinguish God's present activity from any future activity. He had a poetic sense of time in which the future and present merged. However, his subtlety of time, the simultaneity of present and future, was almost lost on his followers. This is evident in his parables where there is no reflection of an apocalyptic view, for example, sayings about the final judgment and the threat of hell are not original to Jesus.

The Kingdom of the Father, for Jesus, is the idyllic society for which people should strive to live in. And there is only one rule: treat and respect everyone like you wish to be treated and respected.

Jesus believed we humans are created by God the Father with a soul and a body. The body will eventually die but not the soul as long as it continues to evolve with greater awareness of its oneness within the harmony of the cosmos.

Jesus believed there is a Light within each person plus within everything created by the Father. The Light is the essence of the existence. But humans have to be aware of it in order to enjoy the Kingdom of the Father.

The Gospel of Thomas

In the Gospel of Thomas, there is no saying dealing with baptism, miracles, crucifixion, nor resurrection. But about half of the sayings can also be found in the canonical gospels. In Thomas they are shorter versions and because of that, biblical scholars considered them older or more authentic. So in reading these sayings, you will realize that they have less to do with theology and more about Jesus' philosophy of life, namely, his vision of the cosmos, how to live in community, and a person's self-knowledge.

Gospel of Thomas

Secret sayings spoken by Jesus and transcribed by Didymos Judas Thomas

1 JESUS SAID

Whoever understands and lives the meaning of my words, your soul will not die

2 JESUS SAID

You must always be willing to seek to find the truth which might disturb your reality.

Then you will be astonished at the wisdom of being conscious of your part in the universe.

3 JESUS SAID

If a religious leader tells you to

look for the Kingdom in the sky, then the birds are first to understand or if he says the Kingdom is in the sea, then the fish are smarter than you.

You must realize the Father's Kingdom is both inside you and outside you. Please know you are a part of every living thing in the cosmos.

If you do not see this, then you miss out on the fulfillment of your life.

4 JESUS SAID

If an elderly person and a newborn were able to discuss the journey of life, then the first would be last and the last, first.

5 JESUS SAID

As you come to understand the cosmos, then you can see it inside of yourself.

6 JESUS SAID

Jesus' disciples asked: Should we fast? How do we pray? What charity should we give? Which diet do we observe?

Jesus responds: (Rather than following religious rituals), do not lie and do not hate. Because being dishonest will eventually become obvious. And treat people how you want to be treated is always the best way to live.

7 JESUS SAID

(Jesus in explaining how the religious bureaucracy makes a law.)

Starting with the premise of how a lion becomes human: it is good if a lion is eaten by a man. And it is bad if a man is eaten by a lion. (*He hesitates ... and smiles.*)

8 JESUS SAID

This story has an important meaning. A good fisherman casts his net in the sea many times. Sure enough he pulls up a lot of small fish. But he keeps trying and one time he searches his net until he spots a big fish at the bottom of the net. Obviously, he throws back into the sea the small fish while keeping the big fish for a tasty meal.

9 JESUS SAID

A farmer goes out to a field to sow

seeds for a new crop of wheat. Some seeds fall on the road and get eaten by the birds. Others land down in the blackberry bushes and are smothered thus being devoured by worms. There are a few that fall into rocky crevasses so they cannot take root. Finally, most are thrown on the fertile ground with the harvest being very successful. (Now you can understand why this teacher is like the farmer. *He laughs*.)

10 JESUS SAID

I have started a fire and am fanning it until it blazes. (A fire of truth pointing out the corruption of the religious elite.)

11 JESUS SAID

Eventually our world will cease to exist, as well as our universe. So our species will not survive. However, enlightened souls will still exist. You are humans consisting of a body and a soul. What do you think you will become when you realize you are in union with the Light ... which is greater than even the cosmos?

12 JESUS SAID

(Responding to his disciples about a successor.) No matter where you are after I am gone, go to my brother, James, for he is righteous and understands my message.

13 JESUS SAID

To whom do you compare me to?

Simon Peter says "a righteous messenger." And Matthew replies "a wise philosopher." Then Thomas responds "Teacher, I am dumbfounded as to how describe you."

Well, Thomas, I am not your teacher any longer. You have heard my message, understand it, and have whole-heartedly accepted it. But I need to tell you something in private.

When Thomas returned to the other disciples after talking with his brother, Jesus, Thomas said "He told me three things but I promised not to reveal them now. All I can say is you might not understand and therefore get angry with us."

(To Thomas in private.) If you fast you will have sinned. If you pray, you will be condemned. If you give to charity, your soul will be damaged. (Don't do these things in public, rather do them in private so you are not a hypocrite.)

It is best when you are visiting other villages that you respect the people and their culture. That way they will honor you as their guest. Eat what they serve you and don't worry about religious taboos. Because it is not what goes into your mouth that defiles you, rather it is what comes out that defiles you.

When you see one who was not born of a woman nor created, fall on your knees and worship with your faces to the ground. For this is your God the Father.

16 JESUS SAID

Some people think I am a peace-maker, but that is not my goal. I want conflicts in peoples' thinking and actions. Maybe families will be divided like fathers against sons and daughters against mothers. People must learn to meditate and live simply.

17 JESUS SAID

I will help you to see what your eyes have not seen. Make you more aware of things you have not heard. And open your heart to a greater depth of feelings.

You ask about the end of time!
Have you found the beginning now
that you seek the end?

Actually both the beginning and
the end are the same circle. When
you understand and realize the
depths of this, your soul will not
die.

(The time when all things were
harmoniously unified in the Kingdom of the Father.)

When God the Father created
all living things in His image, it
was "good." If you disciples truly understand this then even the
non-living stones will show His image. In paradise your five physical

senses become spiritual so your soul can live forever.

20 JESUS SAID

The Kingdom of the Father is like a mustard seed which is the smallest of seeds, but when it falls on cultured soil it produces a large weedy plant. And it becomes a home for many birds.

21 JESUS SAID

(*In response to Mary of Magdala on how his disciples are doing.*) They are like little children playing in a field that is not theirs. When the owner comes to order them out, as a protest they strip off all their clothes and say "here, you can have it all."

If the owners of a house know a

thief is coming, they will be on guard, so when the thief does come they will not let him in to steal their possessions.

The children have not yet acquired their spiritual assets so they have nothing of value except their clothes. As adults who have worked hard to gain insights, I have taught them, they should guard against charlatans.

Listen up, so when death comes like the reaper of the harvest you will be ready.

22 JESUS SAID

These nursing babies are like those who enter the Kingdom of the Father. When they are born they are united body and soul.

However, as persons grow, they must continue to gain greater self-knowledge of being in harmony with the natural world. They must not have biases nor discriminate against others. When you can make your eyes, hands, and feet into ones that are at one with the cosmos, then you can enter the Kingdom of the Father.

23 JESUS SAID

I shall choose only one from a thousand who fully understands my message, and only two out of ten thousand who lives my message as those who will enter the Kingdom of the Father. Because my message is difficult.

24 JESUS SAID

Listen up, this is important. Within every human being there is a Light which can be described as a divine connection with the cosmos. The people who fail to find this inside themselves face a dark future.

25 JESUS SAID

Love and respect each other as you would do to your own self.

26 JESUS SAID

You see a wood sliver in your friend's eye, but overlook the wood timber in your own eye. It is best for you to remove your timber before seeing well enough to remove your friend's sliver.

27 JESUS SAID

If you do not fast from worldly

concerns, then you cannot find the Kingdom of the Father. If you do not observe the Sabbath which is a way to give gratitude, honor, and respect to God the Father, then you will not see His Kingdom.

28 JESUS SAID

I have come into this world to find intoxicated people from worldly pursuits who have no desire for seeking spiritual truth. My soul aches for these people as they are blind and will leave this world dark and empty. Hopefully, I can help some sober up and seek the truth.

29 JESUS SAID

It is marvelous when a person is born to experience life with a soul.

But truly marvelous when an imperfect person's soul comprehends the reality of the Kingdom of the Father.

30 JESUS SAID

When there are three gathered together in a temple, God is with them.

When there are one or two praying but not in a temple, God is with them.

31 JESUS SAID

No prophet is heard in his own village.

No doctor can heal his own family.

32 JESUS SAID

A fortified city built on a mountain cannot be taken nor be hidden.

(Just like a person who has discovered the Kingdom of the Father.)

33 JESUS SAID

Proclaim from the rooftops and light a lamp on a high stand … not under a basket (that you have discovered the Kingdom of the Father).

34 JESUS SAID

If a blind person leads another blind person, they both can fall into a pit. (*Duh, don't follow a hypocrite.*)

35 JESUS SAID

To steal from a strong man's house, you have to tie his hands first.

So don't make it easy for a charlatan to bamboozle you.

36 JESUS SAID

Don't worry from morning to evening and evening to morning about what to wear.

You came into this world without clothes ... so don't worry, be happy.

37 JESUS SAID

You, disciples, ask about being able to always see me, I say take off all your clothes so you are naked and not ashamed. Put them on the ground and trample them like children would. Only then can you recognize the sons of the Living Father, and not be afraid.

38 JESUS SAID

Often you ask to hear me speaking these sayings. Unfortunately, there is no one else to say them, so listen carefully, because in the future you will not be able to find me.

39 JESUS SAID

The Pharisees and scribes have hidden important points about the Kingdom of the Father from you. They personally do not want to do the hard work of understanding so they don't want you to do it either.

40 JESUS SAID

Any grapevine, meaning teaching, that God our Father has not planted is false. It will be pulled up by its roots and die.

41 JESUS SAID

Whoever possess love, will be given more. Whoever does not possess love, will be deprived of what little they even have.

42 JESUS SAID

Realize your life is a journey.

43 JESUS SAID

You know that my actions speak for themselves. I walk the talk. Well some of you like the talk but hate the walk, while others like the walk, but hate the talk.

44 JESUS SAID

Whoever does not respect the Creator nor His Creation, can be forgiven.

Whoever does not respect other

human beings, can be forgiven.

But whoever does not respect, his or her own soul, cannot be forgiven neither in this life nor the next.

45 JESUS SAID

Do people harvest grapes from thorn trees or figs from thistles? No, because the thorn trees and thistles produce bad fruit. So people who say the truth and do selfless deeds are good, while liars and disrespectful people are evil.

46 JESUS SAID

Since the time of Adam to now, all the people who have been born there is no greater one than John the Baptist nor one who deserves more reverence. If you recognize the unborn child in yourself, you

will become even greater than
John in the Kingdom of the Father.

47 JESUS SAID

Here are some thoughts: at the
same time, a rider cannot mount
two horses; an archer cannot
stretch two bows; nor a slave serve
two masters. You have to decide
which is more important. No one
drinks aged wine and then wants
new wine; nor no one sows an
unshrunken patch on an old gar-
ment. You should use common
sense in your thinking and actions.

48 JESUS SAID

If a couple living together in the
same house can live in peace, they

have the ability to overcome any hardship.

49 JESUS SAID

Congratulations to those of you who have found solitude and learned to meditate. You can discover the Kingdom of the Father inside yourselves.

50 JESUS SAID

If people ask, you have become children of the Light and who realize the Kingdom of the Father inside yourselves and thus live in peace.

51 JESUS SAID

In answer to your questions about eternal life and the Kingdom of the Father, they are available to the living now, but I don't think you don't realize it.

You say that 25 Israel prophets have spoken of me, but I say that person is dead. The one who is alive is everyone who knows the Light is in them.

My answer to your question about whether circumcision is useful or not, is simply, if it was useful then the male child would be born that way. What is useful is for each person to make a spiritual convenant with the Father.

Blessed are those who are not burdened by worldly things for they already belong in the Kingdom of the Father.

55 JESUS SAID

If you cannot be free from the demands of your parents or the pressures of your siblings or treat others with respect, you cannot be my disciple.

56 JESUS SAID

Most people see a world populated with only people who do not have a soul. When you realize this, then you can comprehend a world of people filled with Light.

57 JESUS SAID

The Kingdom of the Father is like a farmer who planted good seed in his field. An evil person came by at night and tossed in seeds of weeds. Rather than pulling up the weeds when they were first noticed, the farmer waits until the harvest to separate the weeds from the grain.

58 JESUS SAID

Blessed are those persons who have worked hard to understand their place in the Kingdom of the Father.

59 JESUS SAID

You must discover your inner Light while you are alive, for after you die it is too late.

60 JESUS SAID

See the Samaritan carrying a lamb. He will kill it so he can eat it. You must be like the living lamb and not be eaten.

61 JESUS SAID

Two people go to sleep at night, one awakes in the morning, the other does not.

62 JESUS SAID

Some of my parables seem mysterious. It is up to you to grow in understanding them.

Be generous to the extent that your left hand does not know what your right hand is doing.

63 JESUS SAID

Have you heard the story about the man with great wealth? One day he decided to invest in a farm with a silo so that he could harvest and sell more grain thus making him even wealthier. The next night he died.

Listen to this story...An important man has prepared a dinner party for the town's elite. Before it starts he sends his servant to each of the guests to personally invite them. The first guest tells the servant he has to go collect a debt. The second has to close on a house he just bought and cannot make it. The next guest's excuse is he has to go to a friend's wedding. And finally the last needs to oversee a farm he recently purchased.

The servant returns to his master saying every guest cannot come but they send their regrets. The master instructs the servant to go out to the street and invite the common people to the banquet.

Here is an important story ... A good man owns a vineyard and agrees with the tenants to split the harvest in lieu of rent. When harvest time comes and a portion needs to be delivered to the land-owner, he sends his servant to collect. But the tenants beat the hell out of him instead. A second servant is sent thinking the tenants may have assumed the first was a fraud. He in turn was badly beaten and returns to the master without any fruit. So the owner decides to prove to the tenants he is serious, and sends his son. Thinking they might inherit the property, the tenants kill the son.

66 JESUS SAID

Show me the stone rejected by the builder. It will be the cornerstone of the foundation for the new building.

67 JESUS SAID

Persons who think they know everything, but don't have any self-knowledge, really don't know anything.

68 JESUS SAID

Blessed are those who are hated and persecuted because they can find a place inside themselves where they are safe.

69 JESUS SAID

Blessed are those who are persecuted for their beliefs for they have come to know the Father.

Blessed are those who are hungry for truth for they will be satisfied.

70 JESUS SAID

When you are able to understand the Light within yourself, it will allow you to enter the Kingdom of the Father. If you do not, then you will live in darkness.

71 JESUS SAID

My purpose is to destroy any house of false teachings so that the truth will not let it be rebuilt.

72 JESUS SAID

My answer to the man who requests I divide the estate of his father with his brothers. Why do you think I should be the divider? I do not wish to be the divider.

73 JESUS SAID

The harvest will be plentiful, but there are too few laborers to bring in all the crops. Let's pray the master can find more workers.

74 JESUS SAID

There are many standing around the drinking well, but there is no water in the well.

75 JESUS SAID

There are many standing in front of the door to the bridal suite, but only two single people will enter.

76 JESUS SAID

The Kingdom of the Father is like a merchant who is searching through some goods he wants to purchase. He finds a beautiful pearl. So he sells all his other merchandise and buys the pearl for himself. So if you find a treasure, you should cherish and protect it so it cannot be destroyed.

77 JESUS SAID

I am the Light of creation. A part of me exists in every thing. Split a piece of wood, I am there. Lift a stone, you will find me. If you understand this then you too can acquire the Light.

78 JESUS SAID

Why did you come out here to the desert? Did you expect to see cattails blowing in the wind? Or maybe a man dressed in royal garments? You do know that just wearing elegant clothes doesn't make you righteous?

Miss, thank you for blessing the womb that bore me and the breasts that nourished me. But I say blessed are those who have listened to my message of the Kingdom of the Father and live it. Because this is more important than my mother's womb and breasts.

One who truly understands the world also understands that the body is more than just a physical presence. So the spiritual becomes superior to the physical.

Whoever has achieved the richness of knowing themselves should lead others. But whoever has achieved worldly power should be humble.

82 JESUS SAID

Whoever is close to me acknowl-
edges they are with me in setting
fire to the corrupt establishment.
Whoever is against my message
will not understand the Kingdom
of the Father.

83 JESUS SAID

Physical images are easy for people to see. But remember there is
a spiritual Light hidden in everything. This Light is, of course, a
small portion of our Father's Light
which we will never completely be
able to understand.

84 JESUS SAID

When you view your own physical
image, you are happy. But when

you come to see your spiritual image of understanding your Light, you will be astonished.

85 JESUS SAID

Adam, created by the Father who is the source of all spiritual power and material wealth, is not worthy of those who have found the Kingdom of the Father. And their Light will never die.

86 JESUS SAID

Foxes have dens and birds have nests, but this human has no place to sleep nor rest.

87 JESUS SAID

How miserable our life can be in this physical body. But our soul can be miserable too if we cannot separate it from worldly actions.

88 JESUS SAID

Messengers and prophets will come and offer you some truths. Other truths you already know from knowledge inside yourselves. When they return you will offer to them your truths.

89 JESUS SAID

Why would you ritually wash just the outside of a cup when the person who made the outside of the cup also made the inside.

90 JESUS SAID

Become my disciple, I will help you, I don't give orders and you will find peace and serenity.

91 JESUS SAID

You ask me to tell you who I am so you can believe in me? You make efforts to learn about our religion and how our planet operates, yet you don't want to work at understanding the message I am preaching now.

92 JESUS SAID

If you want to know the truth, you will find it.

In the past I did not give you answers because I wanted you to think for yourselves. Now I am willing to help you understand but you are too lazy to work to find the answers.

93 JESUS SAID

Do not give sacred items to dogs because they will just bury them in a shit hole.

Do not give pearls to pigs because

they will just trample them in the mud.

94 JESUS SAID

One who seeks will find it. One who knocks it will be opened.

95 JESUS SAID

If you have money, don't lend it to someone who can pay it back with interest. Rather give it as a gift to someone who really needs it.

96 JESUS SAID

I have an interesting story ... The Kingdom of the Father is like a baker who mixes the dough with a little yeast and makes many large loaves of bread.

97 JESUS SAID

The Kingdom of the Father is like

a woman carrying a jar filled with flour. While she is walking home, unknowingly a handle accidentally breaks on the jar slowly spilling the flour along the road. When she returned home she finds that the jar has lost all its contents.

98 JESUS SAID

The Kingdom of the Father is like an assassin whose job is to kill an important man. He practices in his own home by stabbing a wall with the sword to test its strength. Then he finishes the job by killing the man.

99 JESUS SAID

I am told my mother and brothers are standing outside waiting for me. But I say to you here who are doing our Father's will that you are more important to me than my family. You will enter the Kingdom of the Father.

100 JESUS SAID

A tax collector just showed me a gold coin and wants us to pay our taxes. Of course, we should give to Caesar what is owed Caesar. And to God the Father what belongs to Him.

(*pausing, smiling*) And give to me what is mine!

101 JESUS SAID

Whoever does not hate your natural parents, as I do, cannot be my disciple.

Whoever does not love your spiritual mother and father, cannot be my disciple.

For my natural mother made me to die, while my spiritual mother gives me eternal life.

102 JESUS SAID

Damn those Pharisees! They are like dogs laying in the cow's manger. They don't eat and won't let the cows eat either!

103 JESUS SAID

Blessed is the person who knows where and when the bandits are going to attack so he can assemble and prepare the armed guards before the attack.

104 JESUS SAID

You ask me to come with you to pray and fast, so what sin do you think I have committed? Or what wrong have I done? You can pray and fast after I am gone.

105 JESUS SAID

Even if you know your father and mother sometimes ignorant people will call you a "son of a bitch."

106 JESUS SAID

When two enemies who disagree can come together and live in harmony, then they have the will to solve the most difficult of problems.

107 JESUS SAID

The Kingdom of the Father is like shepherd who had a 100 sheep. The largest went astray one day. When he realized it, he left the 99 and went looking for the missing one.

After much time and effort, he found the lost sheep and returned to the flock. When he got back he told the wayward one that he loved it more than the others.

108 JESUS SAID

Whoever hears and understands my message will become like me and we will be twins. Also many wonderous things will be revealed to you.

109 JESUS SAID

The Kingdom of the Father is like the landowner who had a treasure hidden in his field that he never knew about since he did not plow his land. When he died, his son inherited the land but like his father, he did not cultivate the fields so he did not know about the hidden treasure. He eventually sold the land to a farmer. The farmer worked hard in plowing and cultivating the field. One day he discovered the treasure and became rich enough by living off the interest of the loans.

110 JESUS SAID

If you find a way to get rich and become wealthy, don't be arrogant nor selfish.

111 JESUS SAID

Hopefully there will come a time when what you thought was reality will not be so. You may experience spiritual love when you recognize inside of yourself the

Kingdom of the Father.

112 JESUS SAID

Damn the body that depends on the soul. Damn the soul that depends on the body.

113 JESUS SAID

I talk about the Kingdom of the Father and you want to know when will it come? You don't understand it will not come as it is already present. It is not over there or over here. Rather it is all over the earth, yet you cannot see it.

114 JESUS SAID

Simon Peter, why would you say that Mary should leave us because women are not worthy? OK, so I will guide her to take on male attributes, but then you will have to acquire female ones. Whoever has attributes of both sexes has a greater chance to enter the Kingdom of the Father.

TAO TE CHING

by Lao Tzu

A twenty-first century English interpretation

by

Jerome

Bonus Works

Other publications by author Jerome include *Thinking Critically*, a compilation of ideas and scenarios regarding philosophy of life issues written for readers to utilize in their own process of thinking critically. And the *Tao Te Ching*, an interpretative rendering of the Chinese classic making it understandable for today's English readers without the need for additional commentaries.

Jerome's books can be purchased from Amazon or his website: writingsofjerome. com

---

From Jerome's Book, *Thinking Critically*

WOULD YOU FOLLOW JESUS?

Would you follow Jesus if you did not think he was God?

But only a man, mighty in word and
    deed
Before God and before all the people?
Or a prophet, or one who hoped to save
    Israel?

For Mary of Magdala, the first to find the
    tomb empty,
She believed someone had taken the
    body
She was the first to whom the risen
    Jesus appeared
But he was still her "Rabbuli," her
    Teacher

When the women told Simon about the
    empty tomb
He rose up, ran to the tomb, and saw
    the linen laid by itself
He went away wondering in himself
Concerning what had happened

His disciples did not believe at first he
    was alive
But only after understanding from the
    scriptures

That he had to rise from the dead
Did he become the Christ, the Son of
 God?

So for Mary of Magdala and all the other
 women
For Simon and the other ten apostles
For the beloved disciple and all the other
 disciples
For years before Jesus died, they
 followed a man

—*Jerome*
 © 2008

WHAT HAPPENED TO MARY(S)?

While Jesus called his God, "Father"
 (*Abba*)
He respected both men and women
 equally
But the two Mary's were closer to him
 than any man.

Mary, the mother of Jesus, taught her
 eldest son compassion for all,

Encouraged his religious studies,
And experienced the ordeal of watching
him die.

She was with him during his ministry to
the unfortunate
She was with him in his rebellion to
bring about a new order
She was with him in his suffering and
crucifixion

She was at the first meeting of the new
movement
When they elected another apostle to
replace Judas
And where Simon Peter took control.

Mary of Magdala was said to be Jesus'
intimate companion
She explained his vision of the Kingdom
of God
To the disciples when they did not
understand.

She was a witness to his crucifixion and
death

She was a witness to his burial
She was a witness to his empty tomb
    and apparition

Yet, she and his mother were shut out of
    the movement. why?
Oh, how different Christianity would
    look today if they had been involved,
Maybe, more like Jesus' vision of the
    Kingdom of God.

— Jerome
    © 2007

TAO TE CHING #14

Look, yet you cannot see
Listen, yet you cannot hear
Touch, yet you cannot feel
These three concepts merged together
Cannot be understood by ordinary men

How can the sun rise but not be bright?

How can the sun set yet not be dark?
How do you name nothing?
    How do you describe formless?

So the *Tao* is called
A formless form
An image of nothing
A thought beyond comprehension

Understand in the beginning there was
    no end
So the unknowable can be known
If you learn to be aware of yourself and
Realize where you came from
This is the beginning of real wisdom
    (*Tao*)

TAO TE CHING #44

Which would you rather have
    Fame or good health?
Which do you value more
    Wealth or happiness?
Which is worse
    Success or failure?

The more you depend on others
    The less self-confidence you have
The more material things you acquire
    The less satisfaction you receive

Know when you have enough
    Otherwise you will not live in
    harmony
Fame, wealth, and success can be ok
    Only if you know when enough is
    enough

Moderation is the key to long life